Unconventional
Classroom
Management

BRENT A. BOGAN, ED.S.

MATTHEW R. OGLES, M.ED.

Published by UC Management,
P.O. Box 12505
Murfreesboro, TN 37129

Cover Art Design by Rachael Ogles

Edited by Andrew Coomes

This publication is designed to provide competent and reliable information regarding the subject matter covered. The authors and publisher specifically disclaim any liability that is incurred from the use or application of the contents of this book.

All web links in this book are correct as of the publication date but may have become inactive or otherwise modified since the time of publication.

Printed in the United States of America.

DEDICATION

Brent and Matthew would like to dedicate this book to the teachers of America. Each and every day you shuffle through paperwork, lesson planning, and hours of grading. It's too often that you sacrifice time for yourself and family in the pursuit of educating our next generation and to that, we say **thank you!**

AUTHORS' NOTES & ACKNOWLEDGMENTS

Brent would like to thank his wife and son for allowing him to always pursue his goals. He would also like to thank his parents for teaching him the value of hard work. Brent's father has written several contributing articles for hunting and trapping magazine's and has been an inspiration to Brent while writing this book.

Matthew would like to thank his wife, Rachael, for encouraging him to always follow his dreams and being his partner in all aspects of life. She has also shown her constant support by spending many hours designing the covers for these books. He would also like to thank his parents for raising him with the foundation to succeed and to always to do your best in everything you do.

Brent and Matthew would also like to thank all of their former, current, and future students for allowing them to grow each year as educators and for allowing them to extend a life-long love of social studies to future generations.

ABOUT THE AUTHORS

Brent Bogan is native to the small farming community of Sabina, Ohio. Brent currently resides with his wife and son in Tennessee. Bogan attended Middle Tennessee State University, where he received a Bachelor of Science Degree in Geosciences, a Master of Education Degree in Administration & Supervision, and an Education Specialist Degree with an emphasis in Curriculum & Instruction. In his free time, he enjoys playing guitar, spending time with his family, and traveling.

Bogan has taught multiple subject areas, has served as a dean of students, and as the department chair of social studies at Riverdale High School. He has been a classroom educator since 2006 and currently serves as the assistant principal of a high performing elementary school. He is continuously testing and applying innovative classroom management techniques to help students learn and improve their academic achievement.

Matthew R. Ogles was born in Tennessee and grew up living in a very small community where he currently resides with his wife. He graduated from Middle Tennessee State University with a Bachelor of Arts Degree in History and with a Master of Education Degree in Administration and Supervision. He enjoys rock climbing, running, creating music, and working around the farm.

Ogles has been an educator of multiple subjects for several years, has served as the department head of Social Studies at his current school, and continues to lead online courses and blended learning courses on a daily basis. He is constantly researching and testing the best techniques in his classroom to help enrich each and every student's life and to share those techniques with fellow educators.

MORE BOOKS BY THE AUTHORS

FLIPPING THE CLASSROOM

TECHNOLOGY DRIVEN TEACHING

FRESHMAN ACADEMY

BLENDED LEARNING

TABLE OF CONTENTS

INTRODUCTION

ONE
BREAKING THE BARRIER • 4

TWO
OPENING ACT • 14

THREE
THE CROWD GOES WILD • 22

FOUR
YOU HAVE TO FAKE IT TO MAKE IT • 37

FIVE
CONSISTENCY AND HOLDING TRUE • 48

SIX
THE SHIVERS OF GROUP WORK • 55

SEVEN
HOCUS POCUS • 66

EIGHT
IT'S JUST BUSINESS • 89

NINE
MANAGING OUTSIDE THE CLASSROOM • 108

TEN
DON'T LET THE LIGHTS GO OUT • 117

ELEVEN
SOME EXTRA TOOLS OF THE TRADE • 129

INTRODUCTION

Teacher retention is at an all-time low. The average teacher only stays in the profession for a few short years. One of the most common causes for people leaving the profession is due to lack of classroom management. Whether they leave by not reaching tenure or they voluntarily leave, few other professions have a high turn-over rate as alarming as teaching.

Many colleges across America have adopted and used the same models and theories for decades when instructing budding teachers the art of classroom management, yet these models and theories have shown little evolution in the techniques of classroom management. The idea of organizing assigned seats, giving direct eye contact with students, and standing in close proximity to those who are talking are just a few of the traditional techniques that are stressed to student teacher candidates. If traditional models are proven to be effective, then why do so many teachers utilize and implement those techniques, leaving teaching all together in the end?

There are several answers to this question. However, the authors of this book have had few problems in their teaching experience with student's misbehaving, while maintaining a classroom that's conducive to learning. This book is a tool to share some of their ideas that sometimes fall into the umbrella of traditional classroom management, with a twist. Other examples of classroom management in this book will totally go against the grain of traditional classroom management. The authors are not saying that you should totally disregard traditional classroom management models and techniques, but are encouraging you to open your mind to alternative methods that have also proven to be effective.

All examples in this book have been time tested by trial and error and utilized by the authors in an effort to maintain a productive classroom that is successfully managed. The authors have experience teaching in rural and urban schools. Matthew teaches middle school students and Brent teaches high school students. Because of the success the authors have had with classroom management, they felt the need to share their unconventional methods with others who may aspire to try something different in their classroom.

The authors hope that you find this book as a beneficial tool; whether you're a brand new teacher who feels like you're drowning in stress and have exhausted all of your options, and need immediate ideas on alternative methods of management, or if you're a veteran teacher looking for something new and refreshing to include into your classroom; the authors hope that you find this book as a beneficial tool. The writers of this book realize that times are ever-changing. Teachers must adapt to meet the learning styles and want to share invaluable techniques that mesh well with today's modern students. There are so many great, knowledgeable teachers who lack successful classroom management. If those teachers had refined their classroom management skills, the students would really benefit from their teaching craft and knowledge. There are so many brilliant teachers who lack the ability to manage the behavior of a class. If you still haven't found success by reading stacks of the traditional textbook theories, classroom management books that are outdated and have been sitting on the shelves of book stores for years, this book may be your saving grace.

CHAPTER 1

BREAKING THE BARRIER

MATTHEW OGLES

Do you like the idea of being eaten alive by sharks? No? Well, goodness gracious, why on earth would you volunteer for it on a daily basis?! The fact is you wouldn't. Yet hundreds of teachers each year describe walking into their classroom this exact same way. They describe it like this because they see their lack of success and feel the eyes of 30 plus students judging them every second. They think of the comics they read growing up where students constantly try to make a teacher's life miserable...tacks on their seats, staples in their tea, laxatives in their coffee...and the list just goes on and on! It's intimidating, confusing, and can honestly be downright painful. While you may not have it quite as extreme as the comics, most teachers do have anxiety of student versus teacher mentality. But how do you prevent this student versus teacher war that has literally been around since the beginning of school? It's easy; break down the barrier that is the great divide between the two groups and let the students see that you are a real person with real interests that are almost certainly similar in some degree to every student you have. Once they see that you have similar interests and are like them, they'll want to work on your team. They won't want to hurt you, disappoint you, or fail you. They don't want to do anything to lose your trust and friendship. It's like this: Think back to your past jobs. Which boss are you more likely to cooperate with and work for? The one you have a great deal in common with and can shoot breeze, or the one that you fear and have nothing in common with? We all know how you answered, and it works exactly the same in the classroom. If you can break down that barrier and show you have common interests with the students and care about them, they're guaranteed to work harder, and for the purpose of this book...they'll behave better for you.

So how do you break down that student versus teacher barrier, get the kids to see you as an interesting person, and connect with them through common interests? There are a multitude of ways to get this connection with your students, and it all starts off way before the students enter the classroom. First off, let's talk about decorating your classroom. Personally, I'm a Social Studies teacher, so I have maps and charts and such throughout my room, much as an English teacher would have grammar rules or a math teacher would have formulas or equations. However, in order to begin to break down the barrier with students, I have so much more in my classroom. I have items spaced throughout my room that represent all the different sides of my personality in order to begin this student-teacher connection. For example, I have my old soccer trophies to relate to the athletes, my academic trophies to relate to the most studious of pupils, music albums I love and adore, musical instruments I like to play, and posters of things and places I love. Integrating objects and decorations show the many aspects of your personality. Make it where no matter who the students are, they'll see something to which they can relate. My students often stay after class just to talk about something they see in my room, and I ALWAYS make time to talk to the students. Once you talk to them, they understand that you have something in common them, and that you also genuinely care about who they are and what they have to say outside of the subject you teach. It breaks down that versus barrier and establishes you in the position as a role model and friend that they want to perform and behave for. Just this last year, I had the *Lord of the Rings* trilogy boxset on my desk, and one day a student who was known for his behavioral issues expressed interest and asked to borrow them. I, of course, let him borrow them, and he finished the series within the weekend. When he came back we discussed the films in detail, laughing and talking as peers. That student saw we had a common interest and that I also took the time to talk to him. He understood I cared about him and we really weren't that different. That student was never a behavioral problem in my classroom again and wanted to work extra hard in my subject because he valued our connection and did not want to disappoint me. He even went on to being one of the stars of the school History Team that I lead. Just show the kids you can relate to them and care about them, and they'll want to perform for you because of the valuable connection you established once that student versus teacher barrier was broken.

The second way to break that barrier also begins before students enter the room: the way you literally dress and present yourself. Some staff are mandated to wear button-up shirts with a tie. While this does no doubt put forth the professionalism to the max, it also cements the barrier for student versus teacher. When students see you dressed like this, they view you as someone that shares few interests with themselves. This can of course be broken down through other strategies if your school requires a dress code like this, but there are ways to look professional while showing your personality and interests in the way you dress. First off, I never wear a suit or tie to school, but opt for a more relaxed and casual look. I'm not saying a tank top with ripped jeans, but nice pants with a stylish button-down shirt and on Fridays, jeans with perhaps an interesting t-shirt. If I wear t-shirts on Friday, I pick ones that represent places around the world that I have traveled to and have a story behind them. The students always ask about them and it gives me the chance to once again show I value the students' interests outside of class and answer them. It reinforces my subject of geography while also showing the students I care about them. The goal is not to look like a student but simply dress to express your personality and make the students realize you are a person too. Just ask yourself, would students connect more with someone dressed as a salesman or someone dressed as a world traveler with the latest fashions? If you are an administrator, I would suggest making at least one day a week casual day to allow students and teachers to connect more as described. I guarantee you'll see a happy faculty that connects with students to ensure better behavior, which automatically ensures better learning.

Now that you and your classroom are literally dressed for success, let's talk about ways to break down the student versus teacher barrier daily. Each day in my classroom, I take a few minutes to tell a story of something going on in my life or a story from when I was their age. The students love my stories and often volunteer to stay late just to hear them. When they hear these stories, they see the similar interests I have with them and the barrier is broken just a little more. And once again, when this barrier is broken, the students are guaranteed to behave better. They also behave better if they know an interesting story is coming at the end of class. I tell them if they behave, I'll take the last few minutes to tell them a story and give them a preview. They wait all class to hear the full story and always leave with a happy face. I am generally more strict at the beginning of the year so they know what I mean by behave, and I'll often hold the story back if they misbehave. This story method increases good behavior in two ways: first, they want to hear a good story, and second, they view you more as a person with similar interests. You may be saying right now, "But I don't have any stories to tell!!" Please. Everyone's life is a story, kids love to hear them, and the more embarrassing, the better! On the way to school, think of an event in your life and practice telling it until you get good storytelling skills also. Kids like good stories, but kids LOVE good stories delivered well. So implement a good story into every lesson and just watch the behavior get better immediately

The next strategy to show you're a person like they are who cares about them is to implement music into your classroom. When doing this step, the more musical variety the better. Trust me, this is a super easy thing to do. For every chapter I cover, my class takes one day to do the chapter review. During these chapter reviews I load up a music streaming service on my computer, and I take requests. Students behave because they know if they don't, then the music is gone, but that's not the main reason. They mainly behave because they know I cared enough about them and their interests to play their music. If I show I care about them, then they care enough to respect me in return. I usually mix in a few of my favorite songs that they probably know also to get them to realize I like the same music as they do, helping to strengthen the student connection bond rather than building the barrier. Students will discuss the music with me, which gives me yet another opportunity to listen to them. It works great every time and is guaranteed to strengthen your classroom management.

What this chapter boils down to is one thing; let the kids know you personally and find a way to connect to every kid so they know you care about them. Trust me, there's a way to connect with every kid you meet. If you connect with them, they'll try harder for you and want to behave because they don't want to disappoint you. This does not mean try to be their best friend, but just simply show you have similar interests as they do and that you genuinely care about them. If you care about them, then they'll care about you.

UNCONVENTIONAL CHALLENGE

Arrive to school early one day a week and take a look around your classroom. Is it a room that will interest students and provoke them to answer questions? If not, take the time to fill your room with conversation starters to help break the barrier with students. It is also good to frequently reflect in your classroom to check for understanding. During your reflection, take the time to evaluate whether the students know that you care about them and whether they see you as a role model. If you're not sure about this, take the active steps listed in this chapter to let the students know you have their best interests at heart.

CHAPTER 2

OPENING ACT

MATTHEW OGLES

I remember back when I was in middle school, I had what I thought was the most awesome teacher ever. He made jokes, had the coolest environment, the greatest lessons, and quite honestly just seemed to have it all. Then it happened...the freakout. One day the class didn't do what he was asking and he lost it...He was like a totally different person. He was yelling, screaming, and truthfully just scary. And guess what. When my buddies and I reminisce about the good old days and that teacher comes up, what do you think we remember? All the cool labs? Nope. All the hilarious jokes? Nope. The awesome posters and environment?? Nope again. All we ever bring up is the freakout. It defined that teacher in the students' eyes for the rest their lives. Now comes the big question. Do you want to be remembered for something like that too? Of course not!! This chapter will show you how to set up a class where you will never have to yell again. In order to have the most success with this though, you will have to establish clear operations from day one and maintain consistency with these operations all year long. This way you can be remembered for your awesomeness and not your awkward fits.

The operations to achieve this must literally start day one, minute one, second one. When students take that first step into the room have an assignment on the board called bellwork. If they enter and have nothing to do on day one, they will assume that this class is easy and they can do whatever they want. Therefore, the teacher must have something for them to do as soon as they walk in the door.

On day one I will stand at the door and instruct them to look on the board for their first assignment, bellwork. After everyone is in the room and seated working, I explain in better details of how bellwork goes. It's a very simple system, and once it becomes a habit, the kids will do it automatically. The system works as follows: they will have one of these assignments everyday as they enter the room. Bellwork activities are usually one or two short answer questions based on the previous day's learning that should take a maximum of five minutes. They keep the whole week's worth of bellwork on a piece of paper and turn it in on Friday for a grade. At the close of the bellwork question, inform the students what supplies they need to get out to be ready for the day. Bellwork in itself isn't the most unconventional activity, but how you use bellwork time most definitely can be. While the students are working on the bellwork, the teacher should not be sitting behind the desk, but rather should be walking around the classroom. While walking around the classroom the teacher should be checking to ensure correct answers and also should be using this time to establish that personal connection that was mentioned in "Breaking the Barrier." As I walk around I ask students about their sports games, their pets, their videogames, their favorite bands, and many, many other things. I use this time to let the students know that I care about them and their interests. They see this connection and, therefore, behave better and do their bellwork because they don't want to lose this connection. When you see the students have finished up bellwork have them check their answer with the person beside them so they can be assured they remembered the material correctly and also discussing it will help them to learn it better.

When you see that the discussion is winding down, you need to have some way to recapture their attention. While some teachers raise their voice and try to dominate the class into submission and quiet down, this is not the way to go. Actually, that is the worst way to go. By doing that you immediately put a negative tone on the class. Instead, think of a cue that can let them know it's time to start back. Instruct them on day one what the cue is and that when they hear it that they should turn their voices off and focus on you. Also, on the first day practice it a few times with the students. The more you practice it at the beginning, the smoother the whole rest of the year will go.

Whatever cue you choose, make sure you stick with it the whole year and are consistent; otherwise, the students could get confused. The cue that is one of my favorites is to simply begin whistling a tune. As students hear me whistle they begin to face me and give me their full attention. I rarely ever have to whistle the whole tune once they understand how the cue works. This cue is elevated voice free, and they all should be.

One of the greatest cues is to have a phrase and when you say it, the class will answer with a responding phrase. For example you could say "Class?" and they will respond with "Yes." You can use any words in the phrases but with this method it forces the students to respond with an action that quiets the whole class down.

Another cue that works is to install a door bell in your room. When you are ready to start, simply push the doorbell and let the students know that when they hear that sound, class is about to start. If you are musically inclined, you can make this even more exciting, bring your instrument in! I play guitar and I know every single time I have strummed one simple chord the students are silent. Kids love to hear music and especially music that the teacher is playing themselves. Just simply play through a few chords and once the kids are quiet, begin the lesson. These are just a few of the cues that I use, but there are limitless potentials so get creative!

I bet I know the questions you're asking yourself right now though, "How do you assure that these strategies will work?" or "How do you reinforce it?" One way is to use what I like to call "Short Film Start." Find a short two minute video (sometimes funny and sometimes serious) to follow the attention cue after bellwork. The students will always want to see the video so they are sure to cooperate with the signals to be quiet. If they do not follow my signals to be quiet after bellwork, well goodbye "Short Film Start" and better luck tomorrow! It will eventually get where students are so excited for the "Short Film Start" that they will remain quiet and calm even after bellwork before the signal. When the "Short Film Start" is over, immediately begin the lesson and no time is lost and transition is perfect. Maintain your pace through the lesson and if you fall back a bit, use opening act cues again to gain attention and begin teaching again. But once the lesson is kicked off right, there should be minimal to no behavior problems throughout the lesson.

In conclusion, you should follow basic operations from day one and start the year off strong! With great expectations, making the students love the opening activities, using personal cues effectively to gain attention, you will have the class focused on your directives in no time. You will literally be the only teacher in your whole school who never has to raise their voice again.

UNCONVENTIONAL CHALLENGE

If you're a new teacher reading this book, make a full-fledged game plan of how you want to start the year. The opening days are the most important ones, and you need to have a plan on how you want to start your class on day one, as well as on a daily basis. Use the bellwork, cues, and short film starts as well as your own opening activities. If you are a veteran teacher and tired of having to spend the whole year yelling, re-evaluate your beginning of the year activities and eliminate any that lead to chaos. If you allow chaos at the beginning, the students will expect it all year long. Let this year be the year you turn over that new leaf and rediscover what it means to love your job as a teacher.

CHAPTER 3

THE CROWD GOES WILD!

BRENT BOGAN

From the Roman Colosseum to Wrigley Field, people have always had a desire for competition. Gladiators entertained tens of thousands of spectators who would root for their favorite fighter to win a battle that would, in many cases, lead to extremely severe injuries and sometimes death. The Romans had such a fascination with being entertained by competition that they actually imported wild, ravaging animals from Africa to compete against the gladiators. In many instances, hungry lions would be placed in the fighting arena of the Colosseum to battle against weary gladiators. In most battles involving "man vs. beast," man would prevail due to the loud roars of cheering from the masses. The lions would become confused, and the gladiators could easily take out the lion.

Today, fortunately for human kind, professional competition is not as violent but still very much unbridled. Wrigley Field and all other modern sporting venues typically have tens of thousands of fans huddling into narrow seats, braving all types of weather that Mother Nature brings on, just to cheer on their favorite teams and players. In many ways, we as humans have not made drastic changes in our love for competition. It's evident when you turn on the television, and there are twenty-five sports channels from which to choose at any given time. If sports are not your thing, you can keep scanning through another thirty or forty cable channels that offer re-runs of game shows or the latest reality television challenges.

If competition is a constant in our civilization, why should we hinder the inner-human desire of competition in our classrooms? The answer...we shouldn't. We're competitive by nature, whether we're viewing it or taking an active part in it. It is in every aspect of our lives. Animals compete for food, water, and mates. Humans are no different when it comes to a biological desire to compete.

The first impression that my students get when they walk into my classroom is that my class is FUN. As soon as you walk into my room, directly next to the door, the students see a bright, fluorescent orange, NERF basketball hoop. Underneath that basketball goal is a large sign that reads, "Geography - Around the World Review." On day one of entering my classroom, the students are intrigued by the goal and the sign. The students typically ask questions about the basketball hoop before I even have a chance to explain that there will be LOTS of games and competitions in my class. Basketball review is great because you can incorporate the questions visually via PowerPoint or Smart Board, you can verbally ask the questions to the auditory learners, and the kinesthetic learners get their blood flow pumping by getting out of their seats to shoot a couple of baskets with a soft foam ball. Unlike real basketball, I have three lines that the students can shoot from: A one-point line, which is basically a free shot right next to the basket for the students who like to play it safe; a five-point shot, which takes a little more skill, and a twenty-point shot for the true risk-takers of the class, as the twenty-point line is nearly twenty five feet from the actual basket. From the outside looking in, it looks like my students are just "playing." The fact is, they are. The best part is that they're playing, having fun, and, most importantly, effectively learning.

A personal goal that I make for myself is to have a review game prior to each and every test and not have one review game identical to the next. Some of these games have been passed on to me by other teachers, while others have been made up while driving to school in the morning. Many teachers believe that games are only effective for the primary school level; however, games are an excellent teaching tool at all levels, including the university level. It has long been a thought of mine that if I could harness my subject and convert it into a video game, every student would have straight A's.

It's important to always set clear expectations prior to playing the game. I have recommended a variety of games to teachers that I have mentored and to student teachers that have worked under my supervision. The consistent commonality in the cause of failure in management during the review game is not setting forth strong expectations prior to and during the game. Prior to beginning the review game, in only one to two minutes, explain the expectations and consequences for everything, from respecting their teammates and opponents to your expectation on the sound level of cheering. Remember, classroom management should be the foundation of your teaching, and although playing a review competition is "fun and games," you cannot lose your awareness of this teacher ideology.

There is such a vast variety of review games that I have my students play that I cannot give examples of my expectations of each, but I have a few ground rules that are universal for all games. One of the first rules that I have is that if something extraordinary happens during the game, they need to control their cheers. I explain to them that if I believe the classroom next door can hear their applause or shouts of excitement, they're too loud. I have a three strikes policy, or "Three-Two-One: We're done!" as I call it. If a team or class gets too loud, collectively as a group, at any given time during the game, they get two warnings. The third infraction results in an alternative review (usually a study guide or chapter review). At the beginning of the year, I'm typically more sensitive to the students getting too loud with their cheering and like to set a precedent for the remainder of the year for my expectations during a game. During this time, I make examples of the "three-two-one: we're done" policy to prove that I will back up my consequences if need be. There is usually one class that will test the boundaries to see what I will let them get away with. I make sure I follow through on my promise of stopping the game. When we transition from the game being cancelled to the hands-on study guide, many students are disappointed. They're not upset with the rule, but they're upset with themselves and their lack of self-discipline. The classes that have experienced losing the privilege of a review game are usually the best behaved during the next review game once they've learned from their mistakes in behavior. You can also put the three strikes on the board and erase them as they lose each strike, so they can visually see that they're losing their opportunity to continue to review the fun way. At the elementary level, you could create a traffic light from colored construction paper. If you stick a green circle onto the traffic light, this will indicate that the noise level is at an appropriate level. When it gets too loud, you can place a yellow circle onto the traffic light. Finally, a third strike would result in red circle being placed onto the traffic light and the game would end, or it could signify that the remainder of the game should be played in complete silence.

Another necessary rule is to make sure that no one criticizes another teammate or opponent. Be sure to have severe penalties in the game for this type of behavior. A common characteristic of a classroom that exhibits great classroom management is one where all students feel safe and comfortable, including the feeling of being safe from bullying. Creating this environment will give students confidence and a feeling of self- worth, at least for the time being in your classroom each day. If the comment is something as simple as, "Gosh, how did you not know that?" I will usually penalize points from the team of the student who made the comment and speak to that student in the hallway towards the end of class to further diffuse a similar situation from ever occurring in the future.

As I previously mentioned, no two review games in my class are alike; therefore, not every review game will have rules and consequences that are alike. My third rule that is consistent among all review games is that during student questioning, I want to hold each student accountable to understanding that particular question and its answer. The way I do this is if a question is missed, I will sometimes call on the opposing team, and I will choose a student at random to answer the same exact question, but I will not repeat the question. This requires the students to constantly pay attention to all questions, not just when it's their turn. The students don't want to let their team down and will stay more alert during the game in order to please their teammates and peers.

Another complaint that I have heard from teachers is, "I have a student who will not participate in the review game." I always have 100% participation during review games. The way in which I achieve this percentage of participation is very simple. I explain that no one will ever be forced to play the review game; however, anyone who wishes to not play will forfeit their turn and the other team will receive two turns in a row to answer questions. No one wants to let some-one lose on their behalf, so they always participate. In this instance, peer pressure is being utilized in a good way. It forces the students who normally would just sit out to not only actively participate but to also study so they don't let their team down. Ultimately, they will effectively be doing what the entire objective of a re-view game is meant to do -- and that is to reinforce their learning.

So you may be asking yourself by now, what's in it for the students? The answer is that it's up to you. I will sometimes buy some inexpensive candy to throw out to the winning team. On some occasions, everyone will get candy just for participating, regardless of a win or loss. (Candy can also be a great lesson-opener, especially if you live in upper latitude areas of the United States, where it's usually dark in the first morning hours of school and your children are half-asleep when school begins). I will sometimes pass out tickets for bonus points on a test, and there are many times I will purposefully not give them anything. There may be some days where the entire class is a team and they're competing against all other class periods throughout the day. In America, we have a society that is stuck on believing that we must constantly receive extrinsic rewards for an accomplishment. In recent years, it has been engrained in students that everyone's a winner. Several years ago, someone decided that we need to do better with raising children's self-esteem. In many cases, this isn't necessarily a bad thing, but it's now to the point where everyone on the tee-ball team gets a trophy. During the last tee-ball game I personally attended, they didn't even keep score to determine a winner. While this is great, it does not reflect real life. I only see my students for a few minutes each day, but I feel it is my duty to have them develop intrinsic value for things they have achieved and accomplished. They need to experience the emotions associated with success and defeat.

Review games can ultimately be your most effective tool in reviewing prior learning. There are several methods of reviewing, but when you create a game, students are going to have fun. I cannot count how many times students have entered my classroom after first period and the buzz has already hit the hallways. The kids know all about the review game and they are stoked about being able to have fun while learning. We shouldn't rob children of the opportunity to play games or restrain them from their inner desire to be competitive. We should instead channel it and use it to our advantage in teaching. It is up to us as teachers to effectively ensure that we have rules in place and that we carry through with those consequences. The worst result would be that the game is cancelled, and they would just pick up where they left off in the form of a study guide or a chapter review. Regardless of the game being cancelled, they're still learning. As Matthew will mention later in the book, if you're not having fun, the students are not having fun. How many people in America get paid to be a game show host? YOU get paid to be a game show host in your own classroom! In addition to being a game show host, you also get to be the executive producer and decide all aspects of the game.

UNCONVENTIONAL CHALLENGE

Review games don't always have to be the typical Q&A style games. Prior to taking midterm exams each year, I have students create their own board games. The theme of their games must relate to a topic that was covered during the first semester. All students receive a comprehensive study guide for the midterm a week and a half prior to the midterm exam. This gives the ambitious students a chance to have a jump start on studying for the exam, but just as important, it gives students questions and answers to incorporate into their board game. The students are required to fill out the study guide, which is information they should have already learned throughout the semester. We review the guide as a class, the students then write out their question and answers cards for their board games, and when completed, we take a day of class to play the games. The students play each board game for 15-20 minutes, and then I'll make the announcement to rotate to a new game. Listening in while playing the games, you can actually hear the progress as the students are playing board games and enjoying learning. Sometimes, I will play the review games with the kids. Every now and then, you will have that one student who spends every waking moment designing the ultimate board game that gives some of the largest game board manufacturers a run for their money.

This project allows students to show their creativity; the repetitiveness of seeing, hearing, and kinesthetically moving game pieces in response to the question and answering appeals to all varieties of learning types. This is one of my favorite projects that I assign students each year. I will show students examples of how they can make game pieces from something as simple as popsicle sticks. Although most students buy supplies for the games, I usually give a speech on how if I were doing this project, I would make it a goal to not spend a dime on making it. I tell the students that I would use a piece of cardboard, popsicle sticks, and the free index cards (which I provide to any student who wants them). Telling the students that I would challenge myself to not spend any money and providing them ideas on how to create a review board game without spending money, give a sense of security to the students who might not be able to afford supplies to make a game board. This also gives them the ability to feel confident about bringing in a game board that they've created with simple objects that were laying around their home. I also explain that if the students are having trouble finding something at the house, they may come and speak with me for ideas. This is another way of inviting the students to speak to me so I can give them supplies if needed.

I would like to challenge you to try the board game review in your class. The student's test scores are almost guaranteed to significantly rise. If you have high stakes testing or a heavily weighted exam, such as a midterm or a final, it's the perfect study tool, and you get to see the creativity of your students. Try it!

CHAPTER 4

YOU HAVE TO FAKE IT

TO MAKE IT

BRENT BOGAN

Before I entered the profession of teaching, I sold real estate as an affiliate broker while attending college. I once sat in a conference that was led by a top, multi-million dollar producing agent. He explained that there are two things that have led to his success, and those two things can lead to any real estate agent's success. The first characteristic that he believed in creating a successful real estate agent was to be a great marketer. You can have all of the knowledge about the industry, but if you don't let the world know that you're in business, you'll never find success in the industry. He further explained that the second trait that a successful real estate agent must possess is that "you have to fake it to make it."

I was astounded that this agent just uttered the words of faking your way to success. I couldn't believe that this guy had attained such a high level of success in the industry simply by faking his way to the top. The phrase, "You have to fake it to make it," kept replaying over and over again in my mind for the remainder of the conference.

While driving home from the conference, I started thinking about the different ways I could begin a strong marketing plan, but I also couldn't let go of the "faking it" phrase. That same day, I was especially more in-tune to observing the billboards while traveling down the interstate on the trip back to my home. Sitting slightly above a line of pine trees to the right hand side of the road, I saw a billboard advertisement that displayed a husband and wife real estate team. The couple both had beaming white smiles and their photo portrayed a confident, happy image. Then it hit me. I now had a greater sense of what the phrase, "You have to fake it to make it," meant.

The real estate agents in the billboard ad may have days when they feel like they've shown the same house 50 times in the past week. In order to not appear redundant, they must fake a smile and pump themselves up to make each house showing as exciting as the first time. They essentially have to fake their enthusiasm when showing the house and beam a shiny white smile each and every time. Confidence is a game changer as a teacher. There will be days when you'll be tired, in a bad mood, days when you have to go into work after your family sobbed about the family dog passing away the night before, etc. As a professional educator, you must leave everything at the door, show your game face, and put on your show.

Wild animals have a sixth sense and can detect fear. Although your students are not animals, they too can identify when a beginning teacher is afraid, nervous, stressed, or irritated. We've all met those nervous substitute teachers whom you pass in the hallway before school starts in the morning. They timidly walk down the hall with a look that clearly says, "I'm lost." You reach your hand out to introduce yourself as they skittishly reach their hand out to extend the handshake greeting. Their apprehensiveness about the day can be felt as you shake their clammy hand and they say in a trembling voice, "It's nice to meet you." Your instant response is, "If you need any help today, my classroom is right down the hall," knowing full well that you'll be making at least one to two trips to save them from paper F-16s flying across the room and random objects being lit on fire. After the quick exchange of greetings, the substitutes take a deep breath and walk on to their assigned classroom for the day.

We also know the substitute teachers who you meet walking down the hall with a confident posture, their head high, and before you can even think about introducing yourself, the substitute already has their hand extended saying, "My name's Debbie, how are you?" Your typical response is, "If you need any help today, my classroom is right down the hall." Their response is, "I appreciate the offer, but I'm sure that I will have no problems." The truth is, those substitutes probably won't have any problems because of the confidence that they exude.

During the first day of school, a student teacher, a new teacher, and even a veteran teacher may be nervous about the day. It's totally natural to feel this way, but you must "fake" your way through the day and display a confident, in-charge persona, or the kids will display a confident, in-charge persona for you, and the results could be disastrous.

When you teach, it's ok to show your personality and who you are. It is also ok to not be the same exact person that you are in the real world. I have met several teachers from different schools in different states that have expressed how they are introverted, and some have even dubbed themselves as "painfully shy." How can someone be shy and be a teacher? It's because they've learned that you have to "fake it to make it." They can turn on the extrovert within themselves, and they take control when it's time to shine. Confidence is critical to creating the impression that you are in charge. If you appear as being meek and soft, you'll never make it to the end of the school year as a successful teacher or disciplinarian.

Another way that teachers can "fake it to make it" is by becoming more in-tune to pop culture. This might not be as difficult for the younger generation teachers as it is for veteran teachers, but it can be important for creating a professional connection to your students. In today's world, students live in a fast-paced environment that is full of technology and multimedia. If the students are talking about the latest movies that you normally wouldn't watch, attend one of the matinee showings of the movie and dedicate a minute or two of class time in the middle of your lesson to tie in how much you enjoyed the movie. Your students will view you in a different light and as a human being, versus a robot that goes home to a library full of textbooks that you read for fun. You should be viewed as knowledgeable and an expert in your subject, but not as a miserably boring person.

Your students have a variety of interests and love telling you about them. On the first day of school, I introduce myself and tell them about fifteen of my hobbies and interests. I intentionally tell them about sports I enjoy playing and watching, how I love the outdoors, riding four wheelers, traveling, my pets, instruments I play, etc. If I simply just said, "My name is Mr. Bogan. I enjoy teaching and love social studies," it is highly doubtful that this statement would help me to make a connection with my students. If I want to create a classroom climate that will gradually allow students to love social studies, I need to let the four or five band students know that I play acoustic and electric guitar and know how to play a few notes on some other instruments, and I need to let the jocks know that I like to watch a good ball game on the weekend and that I played basketball in middle school and high school.

I enjoy a video game here and there, but I have honestly gone a few years at a time without touching a video game controller. However, I tie in video games to my lessons all of the time to make a connection to the gamers in the classroom. Making connections with interests and hobbies of your students can be huge for managing your class. If you focus on incorporating pop culture and connections, it will significantly improve the occurrences of disruptions as well as students becoming unruly in your class.

I always stand in the hallways to greet my students when they enter class. Just having your presence in the hallway can deter fights and bullying in the hallways. Sometimes, you will have students approach you, and they will just want to talk. We're all human and sometimes you will have students that will tell you all about their weekend, and their conversation may involve nothing that you're interested in. You need to act interested. Even if you're really thinking, "I don't care!!" You need to care because the student who is excited to tell you about their weekend could be the next ring leader of misbehavior in your class. Sometimes all it takes to have a "bad" class is one spoiled apple in the bunch for it to spoil all of the apples. Those students will not want to disappoint you if they feel you're on their side and they know that you care about them. Another reason to pay attention is you may be the only person that will listen to that student all day. Everyone needs to feel acceptance, and a teacher should adapt to conversing with a wide variety of personalities. It may be a small thing for you to have a conversation with a student, but it could be the highlight of that student's day.

Positivity is the key to a successful classroom. By speaking energetically and talking highly about the class, the students will feel good about themselves and are surprisingly more apt to follow directives when there is a positive vibe in the classroom. I frequently praise my students on how they had an "awesome perspective" or a "very cool answer." Even when their answers are not even close, I tell them, "That's not the right answer, but it was a very good guess." If they're close to the correct response, I may say, "That's not right, but it's great that you're thinking in the right direction." Positive reinforcement can go a long way when you're teaching. I even explain to the students how they always do such a great job, and I feel that they're going to knock it out of the park with the test on Thursday. The students will want to meet your expectations and will exert more effort into studying. The more comments that you make to boost the self-esteem of students individually or of a class as a whole, the more control on the reins of your class you'll have. Reinforcing that students are valued and that you think highly of their capability will motivate students to work hard and stay focused. More importantly, you'll be able to push your students to reach learning levels that may not have been possible without the extra encouragement. Just make sure that your encouragement is genuine. It took me a few years to understand this, but lecturing on how bad they are and how they're terrible at following the rules won't get you too far. Just like the craft of pedagogy, teachers with great classroom management are not born with the natural, innate ability to have excellent classroom management. It will take practice, time, and effort. By reading this book, it is evident that you're already a great teacher because you've taken the time to read additional resources for improvement. It will also take a great deal of trial-and-error to perfect your own unique style of management.

UNCONVENTIONAL CHALLENGE

At the end of the day, before you tell all of your students to have a great afternoon, ask them if they've seen any good movies lately or if they plan on watching any new movies that are out in theaters. Make it a point to rent or buy a ticket to view one of the more popular movies that the kids are talking about. On Monday, you can talk about the movie, and if you want, you could even tie it into the lesson. Obviously, not all of the students will see that movie, but it will create a great rapport with you and your students.

CHAPTER 5

CONSISTENCY AND HOLDING TRUE TO YOUR WORD

MATTHEW OGLES

Let's imagine a new governor is running for election. He has promised tax cuts, salary raises, better parks, and honestly everything you could want in a new governor. You go to your local precinct, cast your vote and wait. A few hours later your candidate has won, and he is your new governor! However…as his years go by, there are no new parks…taxes have up…and you are still making the same pay. How would you feel?? Frankly, I would feel disgusted and would lose all faith in the governor because he was not true to his word. So tell me, what is the difference in making promises to your students and not following through with them? There's no difference at all!! When you make promises to your students and don't follow through on them, then you lose all credibility and re-spect. The loss of those two things is a recipe for disorder in the field of classroom management. You should always be a man of your word to your students, but this rings especially true when dealing with re-wards and punishments.

You're teaching a lesson and you say, "Guys if you are all good, then we will watch a video in class tomorrow!" You finish the lesson, the kids are great, and they head out for the day. The next day they come in, you start teaching, and then a hand goes up...you call on the student and they say, "Weren't we promised a video today?" You pause for a moment and then respond, "Well, I didn't want to get us behind so we will have to watch one another day." First off, you've lost half the students for that day alone. All their mind is thinking about is why they are not watching that video. But bigger than that, all the students are now seeing you as a liar. The next time you tell the kids if they are good then they will get a reward, they will not change their behavior at all. They will just remember the last time and think, "Why behave better, he's not going to reward us anyway." This I can speak from personal experience.

One year I had bought a new candy called, Espanto. I liked the candy quite a bit and told the kids about it. Naturally, they wanted to try some. I told them, "If you all pass your test, I will bring enough Espanto for everyone!" Well sure enough, everyone passed the test. I was bound to get everyone of them some Espanto. I went to the store...no more Espanto. I went to another store...no more Espanto. Everywhere I went, the same story...No. More. Espanto...I went back to the kids and told them, "I can't find any-more Espanto." I apologized and told them the stores were all sold out and how I must have waited too long after Halloween to get it. Yet, no matter what I told them, I could see the look of disappointment and lack of trust on their faces. I would try different ways to make it up to them, but every time I promised a reward that year at least one student would say, "Sure, Mr. Ogles....just like you promised us Espanto." Breaking one reward promise won't kill your teaching for a year, but every promise you break for a reward, the less your students they trust you and the less they trust you, the more likely they are to misbehave.

Rewards are not the only area in which one should keep their promises though. Keeping promises for punishments is equally, if not more important. If you tell a student or students, who are misbehaving that you will punish them if they don't straighten up and then you don't, they will never take another threat se-riously.

I remember when I was in 8th grade we had a student teacher who was full of empty threats. Almost every day he would ask the class to quite down and then stand by the page button for the office yelling that if we didn't then he would push the button. Some days he would stand there for five minutes just saying, "I'm going to push it! I'm going to push it!" Guess what? He never pushed it. After seeing that he made hollow threats, we as a class never got quiet for him again. Even in the hallway, students would pass each other saying, "I'm going to push it," in a deep mocking voice of the student teacher.

The point of this story is that if you say you are going to punish students and then do not; they will never listen to you ever again. But how can you avoid not following through? It's easy, only make threats on things you know you can follow through with. We knew deep down even as kids that the student teacher would not push the button because it would make him look weak in front of the administration. Pick punishments that the kids know can happen and you can enforce. Threaten isolation, silent lunch, silent lesson, no computer time, or no videos. Pick threats you can enforce and things kid do not want taken away. When enforcing the punishments also make sure that you complete it in a timely fashion. Otherwise the students will think you forgot and not understand why they are being punished when they are. This is almost as bad as not punishing at all. Just remember, if you make hollow threats not only will they not behave, but they will mock you with their friends who might be younger and could make potential problems years down the road.

Being a man of your word is easy; it just takes some forward thinking and a small bit of extra effort. If the kids ever get the sense that you do not mean what you say, then they are sure to act up. Remember when you promise a reward, do it. When you promise a threat, make sure it is possible to follow through with it and to do so in a timely fashion. This will make managing your classroom easier and easier.

UNCONVENTIONAL CHALLENGE

Take the challenge this year to always hold true to your word. If the students see that you follow through with your word, they will respect you more and behave better instantly. To get this kicked off right, make a promise to reward your students this upcoming week and let them know ahead of time. Show them that you reward good behavior and efforts, and that you follow through with it. If you have broken promises to the students in the past, take the next couple of weeks to right your wrongs, and the students will instantly regain respect for you and a well-managed classroom will be on the way. Better late than never in some cases.

CHAPTER 6

THE SHIVERS OF GROUP WORK

MATTHEW OGLES

Group work. Just hearing those words is enough to send chills down most teachers' spines. When they hear "group work," they immediately imagine a wild classroom full of kids yelling and in a state as close to anarchy as a school can get. It is precisely why most teachers choose not to utilize group work at all. Yet, group work can easily be turned into a time when kids are their best behaved! And, not only will they be better behaved, they'll learn more at the same time! So what separates chaotic group work from effective group work? It all lies in the activity that the students are working on, and how clear you've laid out the role of the students. If the students know their individual job and are having fun, group work is guaranteed to be a success in learning and maintaining good behavior.

Successful group work with good behavior all begins with how you divide the groups. Never do the random group divisions where the kids count off for their group or just random pickings. Successful group work has intentional groups. When I divide my students for groups, I always map out the students the day before and try to match the students on their abilities. I try to match my highest achieving students with my students who struggle a bit. I map the groups out so there won't be a super group within the classroom nor will there be a group that falls behind. If you have a super group they will just finish the work immediately, and then proceed to goof off because it was too easy. If you have a struggling group, they will just see they are getting behind, and quit early and begin to goof off too. If there is competition between the groups and you have one group that is just dominating because all the overachievers are in the group, then the other groups give up early. It's when they give up that they start acting up too. The best-behaved groups are the ones that are evenly balanced.

Once you have divided the groups up, make sure that everyone in the group knows their role and knows the idea that a group can't succeed without all members participating. It is because of this that I actually prefer to keep the students into smaller groups of three or four people. This way every member in the group has a particular role. The role of each group member will vary based upon the group activity; but, I make sure to let the students know their own individual role within the group. When the students are doing their group work, the teacher is never to just sit down and just take a load off. The teacher should be walking around the classroom and making sure that the group is working as a team, progressing, and that every student is pulling their weight. When every student knows that they matter, then they are much more willing to participate due to peer pressure, and if they are participating, they are in turn behaving.

While these techniques should be present in every group assignment to get them on the right start, you're probably asking yourself right now, "What are some examples of group activities that will actually hold the students' attention?" Ultimately, this is the most important part of group work. Even if your groups are divided well and the students know their roles, if the work isn't enjoyable or exciting the students will still lose interest and begin misbehaving. In my classroom a day rarely goes by that I don't have the students in groups and that they are excited for group work.

One of my favorite group work activities I use is a year long one. At the beginning of the year I match my students up into groups of three based upon their abilities. I then seat them in their groups and allow them to choose a team name. The name can literally be anything they want, and they love being able to choose it. Next step is that I teach my lesson like normal. However, I always finish the lesson about five minutes early for the group competition. I let them use any notes they took in class and I put a five-question quiz on the board. The students will compete against their fellow groups to try and get the most questions correct. The first group that finishes will get an extra point for being fast too. The students always race through their notes to try and be the first group finished. When a group finishes, I have take home note pages for them to start completing so they don't have a down time to get off track. When all the groups have turned their quizzes in, I begin to rank group scores on the board. Every group gets to see how they ranked against their fellow groups. They LOVE this competition. But while the competition itself drives them extraordinarily well, it is the prize they are competing for that really pushes them. At the end of every section, I update the scores until the chapter is completed. After the last group quiz I always have one group that is victorious because they have the most points. This group wins the Chapter Prize. The prize is different every time. Sometimes the prize is a coke and candy bar, sometimes an awesome toy I've found, and sometimes even gift cards. The prize should be something the students honestly want. After the first chapter is finished and the groups that didn't win see the prize, they work twice as hard for the next chapter and the quizzes in order to get a prize. This works for behavior in two ways; it keeps the students on track during the lesson because they know they are responsible to their team, and it also keeps them focused on the group work because they want to win. If the students are focused constantly and excited to learn they will behave wonderfully. After every two chapters I give the opportunity to swap groups, but even then I still choose the groups myself to make sure they're all evenly matched. This group work activity alone can revolutionize the way your classroom behaves as well as their excitement level on a daily basis.

Another group activity that I use in my classroom and that you should too is a chapter review game. This also has to be used correctly or otherwise will lead to chaos. For group review activities I have a range of different games. I have anywhere from Bluff to Jeopardy to even things as unconventional as Mario Kart. Let us start with a game called Bluff. Bluff is simple;

you divide the classroom into two teams. You then ask team one a question from the chapter. Everyone who "knows" the answer on team one stands up. The trick is they can stand up without actually knowing the answer. A member of team two then calls on a member from team one who he/she feels is bluffing. If the person called on indeed doesn't know the answer, then team two will receive a point for every member standing up. If the person called on does know the answer, team one will get a point for every member standing up. A person cannot be called on twice in a row to avoid "picking" on a student. The kids love it because it adds an extra element to a review game and allows literally everyone to participate because they could stand up for every answer and hope no one calls their bluff. The team with the most points wins, and I usually offer extra credit because I want the team to feel motivated to win. The kids have a ton of fun with this game and are so excited about it and the ability to bluff, that misbehaving is the last thing on their minds.

While Bluff is clearly one of the students' favorites in my room, a spin off on the game Jeopardy works almost as well. Let's say that chapter has four sections. I use each section for a category and the 5th

category is just called "Student Interests." There are questions worth 100 to 500 points in each category and the students get to choose their category and answer it as a team. I always divide the students into four groups so there is never a member that feels like they are not valuable. If a team misses the question, it is transferred to the next team for double points. This makes every team listen carefully because I don't repeat the questions and if they want to get the question right then they have to listen to every team's questions. While this game is more straightforward, it does have its unique quirk to it also. It is hidden in the "Student Interests" category. The students at the beginning of the year all write down an interest and I store these in a container. When they pick that category I draw an interest from the "Students Interests" jar, and make up a question about that interest. They never know what they are going to get when they pick this category! It could literally be anything, but it is student driven and they know it is about what they care about. The kids love this category and are always excited to choose it.

When I do a review game sometimes I divide the class into four teams for a game I call "Mario Kart Review Game." A few years ago my school found a

Nintendo 64 system stored away in a portable. The school was just going to dispose of it, but I stepped in and said that I would like to use it in my classroom. While most staff members were puzzled as to how, it has become one of my leading games. I took the system back to my room and hooked it up to the projector and went and got an old game called "Mario Kart." I have always loved the wacky races on it and knew the kids would also. So what I do is, I have the system hooked up as the students enter the room, and they immediately know something fun is up. I tell the kids that we will have a special video game time at the end of class if they all behave during the review game. I then divide the kids into four ability-based teams, and then go through a normal review game of choice. After 15 minutes I pause and tell each team their total score so far. Then each team is allowed to bet their points on a Mario Kart race. Whatever they bet they get added to their score if they win, and whatever they bet subtracts from their score if they lose. I have the system loaded up already and the four racers come up, one from each team. They do a two to three minute race as their team cheers them on, and then back to their seats for 15 minutes of more review questions. After the 15 minutes, it's time for yet another Mario Kart race. After three series of races and three rounds of questions, I total the points and the winning team gets extra credit points for their test the next day. I know this may sound chaotic, but the kids are so excited about the races that you could hear a pen drop because they don't want to lose the game time. I've had multiple kids come up to me and say that Mario Kart Review Game is literally the most fun they have ever had in school. This is quite a complement because they have been in school at least eight years by the time they have me!

What group work boils down to is basically making every kid feel their importance and make the activity so fun that misbehaving does not even cross their mind. The best behavior plans are not reactive but rather proactive. If you divide the groups correctly with individual roles and have a fun game planned out, you can kiss behavior problems goodbye during your class.

UNCONVENTIONAL CHALLENGE

During your planning for the upcoming week include at least one group work activity. Make intentional groupings, establish clear roles, and most of all make it fun! Once you see how group work can enrich your classroom without being chaotic, plan the next week with two group work activities. Keep increasing the number until you can have a whole week of group work activities. Once you reach this comfort level you will be able to plan and handle group work activities on the fly and can have the fun well managed classroom you have always dreamed of.

CHAPTER 7

HOCUS POCUS

BRENT BOGAN

Magicians creating illusions have long been an audience favorite. Magicians have been wowing people by showing them an empty hand and by exclaiming the words, "Hocus Pocus," and with the flick of a wrist, a rabbit or other large object mysteriously appears where there was once an empty hand only seconds before. Tourists in Las Vegas will pay hundreds of dollars for a ticket to see a magic show that's receiving the greatest buzz on the streets.

"Hocus Pocus," is a phrase used by magicians to indicate that a change is getting ready to take place. Changes in your classroom are a must for successful classroom management. Call it what you will -- differentiated instruction, transitioning, or a segue -- changes are one of the most important necessities to your classroom.

If you were to look at each of the ten chapters of this book as essential classroom management techniques for your room, this chapter would be included as one of the top three most important techniques for effective classroom management. While all techniques and methods are equally important to ensure success, if you don't have variety, you'll never maintain the attention of the students.

We've all had that teacher who constantly does the same thing, hour after hour, day after day. I once had a teacher who would make us take notes Monday through Thursday, and on each and every Friday, we would test over the information that we wrote the previous four days. I will never forget the day when we watched a video in his class. Nearly twenty years after taking his class, I still clearly remember the moment of excitement that was felt throughout the class when he made mention of a change to our typical, redundant learning schedule. Unfortunately, the video was in black and white and was on an old projector that had two reels moving through the scenes like a scratchy, homemade movie. I'm sure the teacher had discovered the video reels in the back of a dusty, old janitor's closet where the movie reels were covered in thirty years' worth of dust. But to us as students, it didn't matter. What mattered was that for one, solid class period, we didn't have to suffer through the same exact lesson that we came to expect like clock-work.

At this point, you may be thinking that the authors are completely iconoclastic towards traditional pedagogical methods, but nothing can be further from the truth. Throughout the book thus far, you've seen a wide variety of unique methods that have been extremely successful in our classrooms, but we still follow most of the fundamental methods of handling our classroom management. We simply modify many of the traditional methods for the modern-day student. It's important to focus your lessons on getting students on their feet and out of their seats. Sitting in a seat all day not only creates boredom, but the students will lose attentiveness and may begin to act inappropriately due to physical and mental discomfort. You probably remember learning about Maslow's Hierarchy of Needs in high school and how a human must meet physiological needs prior to obtaining the next level on the pyramid. This applies to student learning, just as it applies to any other situation. Teachers can incorporate learning stations where the students have to move amongst the room in order to discover new content. Teachers can also use inquiry lessons to prevent exhaustion of sitting in a rock-hard desk. No student should be prohibited from getting out of his/her seats after sitting for thirty to forty minutes at a time. Intentionally design your lessons to allow students to get on their feet, interact, and get their blood flowing. We all know that the correlation of exercise and blood flow to the brain can have significant, positive results for memory and retention, but rarely do most teachers place emphasis on movement in the classroom. If you're teaching the difference between coniferous and deciduous trees, don't just show them pictures of the differences. Walk your students outside for a mini field trip around the school to discover the varieties of trees.

Technology should be a major focus for anyone who is teaching in the twenty-first century. If you're not using technology, you might as well be teaching to the wall in the back of the room. When the students aren't at school, they're constantly using technology in some capacity. Texting, video games, the internet, and television are just a sampling of the many ways students use technology. With all of the technology that is marketed to teachers today, it is so easy to incorporate it into your class. If you're a veteran teacher who has resisted introducing forms of technology into your room, you're really hurting your students.

Teachers who adapt to change and include technology in their teaching captivate the attention of their students and reduce boredom. Some school districts may not have the funds to afford a wide variety of technology. There are many corporations who offer grants and would be glad to have a tax write-off for helping out their local school. In most cases, you'll have to apply for and write a lengthy application to receive a grant, but many grants can be awarded by simply filling out a one-or two-page form. It's just a matter of applying.

You should also focus on asking as many open-ended questions as possible and open the floor to as many students as possible. Not only does this promote higher-order thinking, it keeps students alert and involved. Another positive effect is that many students seek attention at school because they may not receive it elsewhere. Many students don't care if they receive that attention in the form of inappropriate behavior, or by answering questions, or by sharing their thoughts, opinions, and answers in class. If teachers opt for the latter, they could be eliminating the desire for a student to misbehave in order to receive attention, and ultimately eliminating disruptions in your class. Many modern pedagogy theories are leaning towards the idea that the students should discuss the subject matter more than the teacher speaks about the subject matter throughout the school day. So this particular method works well for classroom management as well as learning outcomes.

When a student can actually teach the material, they have developed mastery of the content. A great way to regularly teach mastery is to have students give presentations over a particular subject within a chapter or unit of study. A way to eliminate redundant presentations is to have a variety of methods in which the students present material. For example, in a social studies course, you could have the students give a newscast presentation over a particular country, versus just presenting a list of facts or reading current event articles from a newspaper. You could have a group of four students present on a country of your choosing. Then, take one or two days in the computer lab to allow students to research their country. By visiting the computer lab, you're using technology and a change in scenery from the regular classroom, which really breaks things up for the students. On the day of the presentation, one student could discuss the weather trends and conditions, the second student could discuss sports, the third student could discuss cultural trends of the country, and the fourth student could present the current events/news of the country. This project allows creativity, acting, and an excuse to dress up for school (every student enjoys dressing up if it's not the norm – just make sure that dressing up for the assignment is optional for those students who may not be able to afford the dress clothes for dressing up). This method uses technology, allows peer-to-peer teaching, and best of all, teaches mastery. You can incorporate interactive presentations in every subject. Just use your imagination with each unit that you teach to brainstorm how you will create a non-traditional presentation tailored for your class.

Year after year, city after city, a very famous country music entertainer named Garth Brooks consistently had record-breaking attendance at most of the venues where he performed. How did he do it? By releasing new songs, having a new stage set, and changing the entire show each time there was a new tour. People continued to return to his shows and flock by the thousands to see how the shows had changed. Garth certainly has great songs but what really drew his audience was the one thing that is a constant, and that constant is change. Regardless of entering the stage through a baby grand piano lid or if he was "flying" by a guy-wire onto the stage across the crowd who had anxiously awaited his arrival to the stage, you never knew what to expect from one show to the next.

Similar to Garth, you should focus on adapting the same philosophy of keeping the suspense of your students high. Changes should not only take place throughout a single day, but the changes should take place from one day to the next. Unless there is a scheduled test, your students should always have to keep guessing what type of lesson you will be presenting, and more importantly, how the lesson will be presented.

In addition to planning transitions, it is imperative to have spontaneity. The more you have it, the more natural it will become. I once had two box tops that belonged to a couple of printer paper boxes for the social studies department. I had placed them on a back table during my planning period and had simply forgotten about them. After my planning period, students began filtering into my classroom. Then one student pointed over to the box tops and asked, "What are those for?" I knew the box tops were for the top of the paper boxes, but my response was quickly, "Once class begins, I'll explain what they're for." As I had to quickly think about how I would incorporate using the boxes in my class, I finally devised a plan.

The students took a seat and immediately after the bell work, I explained to the students that it will be to their benefit to make sure that they pay extra close attention to today's lesson because there are some prizes up for grabs at the end of the day for those who are attentive. You should always include a strong lesson closure at the end of your lesson. Every truly great movie has a strong ending, and your lesson should be no different. On this particular day, prizes would be included as part of my lesson closure.

I knew that I would need to put some prizes underneath the two box tops, but now I had 35 students sitting in class. How could I put anything underneath the boxes without 70 eyes noticing that I was putting something underneath? The solution was that I would sneak the prizes underneath the box tops during the next transition in the lesson. I would quickly move onto the next part of the lesson by setting a good pace, according to how long the students were engaged in each lesson. The first part of the lesson involved their focus on the front white board. The next objective of the lesson evolved to looking at a skills activity on their desk. The students were so focused, that I had an opportunity to go to the back of the room and place some prizes underneath the boxes while the students had their eyes faced towards their desks, working on the hands-on assignment. I placed a used pencil that I found on the floor under one box, and underneath the other box, I placed "bonus card tickets" (which I'll explain later in this chapter), candy, and a t-shirt (I had a free t-shirt that was left over from a club that I used to sponsor at my school – thanks to a printing company that gave me more shirts than we had ordered).

I transitioned to a couple of other variations of the lesson for further reinforcement, and towards the end of class, I explained that if the students could answer three consecutive questions correctly about today's lesson, I would let them choose a box top and everything underneath that box top. When I asked for the first volunteer, it seemed like the entire class raised their hands to answer the questions. Throughout class, the students were extra focused on learning and because they knew a prize was involved, there were no discipline problems whatsoever. The students were also actively engaged in the learning because of the constant changes taking place throughout the lesson.

I called upon the first student and asked three questions. She quickly blurted out all three answers correctly (remember that this is a form of lesson closure; although at this point, an unnamed prize is at stake). I allowed that student to choose a box. The student nervously thought about her important decision in choosing a mystery surprise that would be awarded in front of the entire class. The student said, "I will pick Box Two." I placed my hands over the box and said, "Are you sure box two is your final choice?" With a bit of hesitation, the student stuck to their original decision. I excitedly lifted up box two and yelled out the prizes: bonus card tickets, five different types of candy, and a t-shirt. That student can wear the shirt to school with bragging rights, and a story of how she paid attention in class to win that shirt. Imagine the story that student will tell her parents at dinner that night. The parents may ask their child, "What did you do at school today?" She replies, "I won a t-shirt, candy, and bonus card tickets. I won it all because I paid attention and learned."

The next student I called upon had no other choice but to choose Box One after successfully answering three questions about the lesson. I placed my hands on the box and said, "Are you ready for the prize?" I then lifted the box and explained, "You get a used pencil that I found on the floor, and in addition to this wonderful prize, it looks like there are bite marks on the pencil where someone has obviously chewed on it!" I let the student believe that this was the prize for about 30 seconds before explaining that he too would receive bonus card tickets, and he could come up to the candy bucket to grab a handful of candy (unfortunately, I didn't have an extra shirt, but that's the risk of choosing the random box top game). There was excitement, a little bit of humor, and it was something that was spontaneous and not typical from day to day. Practice your focus on random, spontaneous teaching; it can only enhance the lesson you had already planned for the day.

Spontaneous changes can sometimes be as valuable in learning as the ones that are planned. There are so many examples of how I've had spontaneous changes in my class. Another example I can think of was when my wife found a rubber "bouncy-ball" that was in globe print at a local general store. I brought it to school, not necessarily knowing what I was going to use it for. Because change is a constant in my classroom, a few students approached me after walking into my classroom prior to first period, noticed the ball on my desk, and asked if it was for a review game. I didn't want to lower the student's excitement, so I quickly said, "Yes, it is for a review game." Now, I had the task to think of a review game involving that ball.

As the bell rang to begin the school day, I shut the classroom door and turned on the television for the morning announcements. During this time, I created a brand new review game. The title was very cheesy, but at least it was something. It was called, "The Thinking Ball." At the end of class, during the closure, all students had to stand up, and I passed the ball to a student in the center of the room. Once the student answered a review question, he/she passed the ball onto someone else, and then took a seat. For the first question answered correctly, the class received one point, and the next correct question was doubled to two, four, eight, sixteen, etc. If they could score 64 or higher before the bell rang to end class, I would give each student a bonus card ticket on the way out. It was a unique, quick way to cap off the lesson, and once again, it was different than any other day. You could also create review games that allow an entire class to become one team. They will compete against other class periods throughout the day and the class period with the most points at the end of the day will win.

Rewards should be both extrinsic and intrinsic; however, one extrinsic reward that I created for motivation and to give the students a sense of self-accomplishment is "Bonus Card Tickets." I print off tickets that have a unique design that couldn't be easily replicated, pass them out for answering difficult questions and as a reward for winning review games. The value is five points, and they can staple one to each test for extra credit. The only way to receive them is by staying attentive and studying. By the first month of school, I make it a point to try to give bonus card tickets to everyone, so they can experience the pride and power of five extra points that they can apply to any test. Students love having a tangible ticket that they can hold in their hands as a result of studying. That ticket has more than the value of accomplishment -- it has the value of five extra points.

Students love to visually see their progress and accomplishments. Writing the daily objectives on the front white board has several benefits. The first advantage of listing the daily objectives is that it looks good and professional when you have an unannounced classroom evaluation. It helps you stay on track of what you're teaching, but most importantly, it shows the students what they're learning, what they've already completed, and what is still ahead for the day.

If you have a particularly difficult class, and there are not one or two identifiable students who are the nucleus of disruption, one way to manage that class is the elimination of an objective. It's not a punishment, but an award. For example, if you were planning on covering six objectives, place a seventh objective on the board before school starts. The seventh objective can be a chapter review, a quick worksheet, or anything that will not take a great deal of time, but goes along with the lesson. By choosing this extra objective, you can explain that if the class follows the rules, and if everyone is working hard and paying attention, you will eliminate an objective. If the class does not reach your behavior expectations, you will keep the objectives as is. You should always choose an extra objective that will tie into the actual objectives but is not critical they complete that objective.

What I have found is that some of the worst-behaved students are the ones who are the most attentive when I use this strategy. At the end of class, if everyone follows the rules, I congratulate them on doing a great job, I remind them of how awesome they are, and then I erase that last objective, so they can visually see their accomplishment of following the rules. The pride that the students have in themselves for behaving and knowing that they were the ones responsible for the elimination of the objective is tremendous. I never had full intentions of giving them that objective in the first place (although they didn't know that), but if overall, the class had talked and there was a general lack of focus, I would explain that they will have to stick with the original assignments on the board (which sometimes results in homework because you ran out of time with the original lesson objectives). It will not hurt them to do the extra objective, but it's a great reward when it is taken away. By trying this, you will actually see the class self-manage itself. I always integrate a group activity into each of my lessons, and this is when the noise level can sometimes get to a level that I deem unacceptable. When the students under-stand that an objective could be eliminated, they will typically remind one another to not get loud.

For elementary and middle school levels, you could give an ice cream sundae party. You could place a letter on the board for each day that the students meet behavior or academic expectations. For example, if the students followed the rules of the classroom on Mon-day, you could place an "I" on the front board. On Tuesday, you could place a "C" on the front board, etc. Once the students have spelled "Ice Cream Sundae Party," you could go to the local supermarket and pur-chase items to have an ice cream party during the last few minutes of class one day. For each day that the class does not meet the expectation of following the rules of the class, you could even take away a letter, which will essentially put them back two days. Once again, I'm not a fan of punishing an entire class, but this is an optional reward for good behavior and not necessarily a punishment.

Teaching from bell to bell has always been pushed. There is nothing wrong with that, but occa-sionally it's good to incorporate conversation that deals with asking students about their weekend or a big game that they had the night before. Teaching from bell to bell includes getting to know your students. This will enable you to know how your students are doing and will give you a real gauge on how your students live are going, which in turn has a great impact on their motivation for learning. When students return from a long break, the one single thing that they have on their mind is to share what they did over the weekend or break with their friends. I explain to my students that if they follow the rules, work hard, and pay attention, that I'll give them the last minute or two to talk about their break. If you didn't have to stop the class for disruptions, give the students back the minute or two that you didn't have to spend reprimanding students and explain to your class that since class time was not wasted on disciplining them, you will take the last minute or two letting the students talk about their weekend while they pack up their backpacks up for going home or to the next class. The kids will love it. You'll only strengthen your management in the long run because they will gain more respect for you by allowing them to express themselves as individuals. The real benefit of this is that you will get to know who your students are, which will help you pinpoint where your students are coming from and who they are – especially those who misbehave. Make an effort to talk with as many students as possible about their break. This is a great way to get to know who your students are, which will ultimately help you with incorporating real life examples into your lessons to better suit the learning needs of students. The students will feel that you value what they did over the break, and displaying respect towards your students begets receiving respect from your students. If you teach a rigorous lesson well, eliminating the last minute or two every once in a while really won't make much of a difference. Trust me, it seems counter-productive towards learning, but your test scores and student achievement will not suffer from this. Just don't make it a daily habit. After a long break, you could even tie in a quick writing assignment of what they did over the break. The students really just want to share their experiences. Even if you don't teach English, writing across the curriculum is great practice for every grade level and every subject.

Throughout my teaching career, I have heard multiple times that an individual's attention span is equal in minutes to their age. For example, if you have nine-year-old students, they may usually only pay attention for nine minutes before a transition needs to take place. My hat goes off in respect to kindergarten and first grade teachers, where the majority of students are only five and six years of age. By keeping this in mind, your class will not only be free of boredom, but your students will be more successful at lesson retention. Variety will keep your class environment vibrant.

UNCONVENTIONAL CHALLENGE

The next time you teach, if your lessons are longer than 20-25 minutes, try shortening each lesson and add on an additional transition or two. Document the differences that you notice with the extra transitions. Were the students more attentive? Was the change in pacing more enjoyable for the students?

If you have trouble filling up the entire class period or day (depending on if you teach elementary or secondary school), always carry alternative "thinking" lessons. For example, you could find some riddles on the internet and pass out candy to the students who answer questions. It's almost like a way to "reset" or freshen the students' minds. Once you pull the students into your subject, you take a break to solve some riddles, which still involves the practice of logic and analytical thinking – or left brain thinking. Then, you can resume the lesson of your subject. The students will really enjoy taking a break and attempting to solve the riddles.

Another activity that has proven to be successful is the reward of watching video clips from the internet. I'm talking about one-two minute video clips that are relevant to the topic that is currently being covered within a unit of study. You can use videos as leverage. Explain to the class that you will show two video clips at the end of class if things go well and everyone stays focused on learning. It's a real treat to the students, and the quick video clips can really make the lesson become more concrete to students. If things don't go as planned or if there's too much "chit-chat" among students, simply tell them that they now only have one video clip left at the end of class and that you took away the one that was the coolest. If they talk too much a second time, take the video clips away entirely. The next time you offer this particular incentive, they'll be more apt to stay focused and will not want to miss out on the videos. It's still educational, it's enjoyable, and videos usually make the learning more concrete to students. You can teach the students about "the running of the bulls," but when you show them a video, it makes it all comes together for the student.

CHAPTER 8

IT'S JUST BUSINESS

BRENT BOGAN

Many colleges of business throughout the United States will teach their students that business should stay just business, and anything personal should not get involved. Being human and treating people as such while simultaneously being in the quest of success in pursuit of the almighty dollar should be compared to oil and water. While some of the most successful corporations don't adhere to this philosophy, many successful businesses wouldn't run a business any other way. We see this on an almost weekly occurrence in the news. Hundreds of employees are cut from the payroll of a downsizing corporation, while the CEOs continues to rake in their comfortable five million dollar salary per year, not to mention their bonus of several hundred thousand dollars.

Just as many successful businesses don't let their emotions get involved while keeping their eye on the prize, teachers should not let their emotions get involved with their ability to teach and discipline students. With the ever-increasing amount of standardized tests being mandated and introduced to schools, understanding growth margins, annual progress statistics, and comprehending the concept of outliers seems to be intertwined with business lingo. Key phrases that you now commonly hear in collaborative in-service meetings involving education are those that formerly would only be used in a business conference. Similar to businesses, teachers are regularly tabulating grades just as an accountant tabulates income and expenses, staying involved with e-mailing their customer base (parents), and marketing interest and appeal to students in the lessons. It's sad, but this is the new reality of the modern school. We must understand our students' past achievement to understand how to gain progress for future testing, similar to how businesses must understand prior consumer buying trends to predict new products, determine future sales projections, and maintain positive growth margins

One of the most important things you must do as a teacher when you begin teaching is to not just convince, but prove that you are the teacher and, ultimately, you are in charge. While you need to convey the message that you're in charge, you should also let the students know that everything you're doing is for the benefit and betterment of their education. After all, the whole point of effective classroom management is for the purpose of student learning. At the beginning of the school year, my school will typically have a short 2-3 hour walk-through, to allow students to tour the school, become familiar with their new teachers, and to get accustomed to waking up early after a summer full of late night marathons of playing video games and texting friends until they fall asleep. On this short day, I explain to the students that the first full day of school will be the most important day of the school year and that they want to make sure they bring a pen/pencil and paper to take notes on this important day. I explain that this day will determine what type of year they will have in my classroom, further explaining that if they pay attention and adhere to what I'm going to discuss, they will thoroughly enjoy this class and it will be a smooth year for them. By explaining this early on, it builds anticipation for what I will be talking about and the topic of discussion is my classroom rules.

On the first day, I lay out the five basic rules for the class. I have multiple consequences for the rules, and I explain that if the students acknowledge the rules, there will be no problems. However, breaking the rules could result in a meeting with their coach or club sponsor (many students will be involved with at least one sport or club), a meeting with their parents, or lunch detention (the students obviously still eat their lunch, but it will be under my supervision without the luxury of talking and hanging out with their friends). All students are different and they may have a parent or guardian that will not enforce any punishment by conferencing with the parents about their child's misbehavior; whereas, that same student may be very much concerned about you talking with the football or volleyball coach. As mentioned in Chapter 1, once you establish a professional teacher-student relationship, the student will usually not want to disappoint you. Until you reach this relationship with your students, parental and coach conferencing could be the alternative in the meantime.

One thing that I mention to the students on day one is that "I will never send you to the principal or discipline dean's office unless you're in a fight or if I feel that you're a safety threat to the class." I explain that I can do anything the principal and discipline dean can do. I have the ability to give you detention, I can contact your parent, I can send you into isolation in the hall to complete your school work, etc. I usually get a lot of shocked faces when I tell the students about not sending them to the office. To this day, I can count on one hand how many times I've had to send a student to the principal's office. My philosophy behind this is that if you send a student to the office, you have lost all power, authority, and potentially respect from that student. It unconsciously shows students that you do not have the ability to discipline children and you must send them away to have someone else do it for you. Sending a student to the principal's office is not a necessity and should only be done as an absolutely last resort. Students fear the idea of being sent to the principal's office, but I want my students to fear the idea of breaking one of my rules. When you speak to students privately in the hall, you can usually get to the bottom of their behavior. Plus, if you don't send a student to the principal or discipline dean's office with the exception of dire emergency situations, the principal/discipline dean will know that you're not "crying wolf" the day you may really have a need to send a kid to the office. They will know that it must be a serious situation if you're sending a student to them. Try to focus on developing a reputation where you don't send students to the principal's office unless it's absolutely necessary.

When I explain the rules to my class, I keep them short and to the point. Your rules can always vary depending on your personality, needs, and grade level, but mine are as follows: 1. Raise your hand to gain permission to speak. 2. Stay seated (the students are constantly out of their seats throughout the day while completing various lessons but they need to understand that they should remain seated until they're instructed to get up). 3. Respect yourself and others. 4. Be prepared. 5. Be on time. These five rules are such an integral part of my teaching that I regularly review these with the students. After any long weekend, holiday breaks, or if there is ever a long duration where I haven't revisited the rules with the students, I make a point to do so.

In my last fall semester of college, I substitute taught to receive experience in an actual school setting. I substitute taught elementary school students, middle school students, and high school students. During one of my assignments as a substitute teacher, the classroom rules of a particular teacher caught my eye. The teacher had over 15 rules for her classroom. Some of the rules overlapped themselves, but what was more disturbing was the fact that I let alone a class of 10-

year-old students wouldn't be able to remember 15+ rules. One of the rules was "Do not stand near the teacher's desk. This not only sends a message to the students that they're devalued to not even be able to stand next to the teacher's desk, but it's also too specific of a rule. Another rule that is clear to my memory was a rule to not throw away paper until the end of class. While this is a great procedure, it should be kept as just that -- a procedure. My 3rd rule is to respect yourself and others. If I were to implement this procedure into my classroom, it would certainly be in the "catch-all" rule of respecting "others," as well as conforming to my "stay seated" rule. The rules that you devise for your class should be able to be used for a wide spectrum of situations, but your rule list should be short and sweet to not confuse students.

I had a great mentor in my early years of teaching who taught government. She actually had her students create and vote upon which rules would be enacted for the class. She explained that the students would usually take more pride in the rules because they created and voted the rules to be the law of the classroom. This is just another great idea that could easily be implemented in any classroom, regardless of the subject or grade level. You could also establish one or two rules that are mandatory prior to the rule addendums that the students will create, just in case you have a class that has ridiculous expectations.

Sometimes a teacher has specific procedures. I have a system of students turning in papers into certain trays and even a process for how to title an assignment, but a teacher should differentiate a rule from a procedure. Procedures are daily tasks or habits that the students should develop and adhere to; whereas, rules are the law of the class and have consequences if they are not followed or are broken. Your rules should be fair, they should be equitable among all students, and you should always follow through on the results of breaking one of your rules. You might not realize it, but your students are continuously studying your mannerisms and will test you, especially in the first few weeks of school, to determine what they will be able to get away with and how frequently you will back up your rules and their consequences. This is a critical time to make sure that you don't make empty threats and that you follow through with your rules. Be quick to take action and administer a consequence when a rule has been broken.

I explain to the students that the rules have been created and are set in place to help them. For example, I explain rule #1 – Raise your hand to gain permission to speak. If I ask an interesting or intriguing question and 15 students are yelling out the answers at once, I will not be able to hear what they are saying, and it will delay class. I further explain that it may not sound like a big deal, but if it happens ten times during class, that could equate to a total of 10 minutes of class being delayed. If that occurs, I explain that anything we didn't finish would have to be sent home for homework. By establishing the "raising your hand" rule, it's to help the students avoid additional homework due to delays; plus it's just respectful to raise your hand and patiently wait for an individual turn to explain an answer or ask a question. Focusing on a hidden curriculum of respect, organization, and punctuality will only help your students through different aspects they'll encounter later in life. You should create rules for the benefit of the students and then explain and justify why the rules exists.

People follow behavioral cues of others and make decisions to determine their behavior in certain situations. The first time I attended a professional hockey game, I didn't have a clue what was going on. I understood the basic concept of the game, but at the time I didn't know the difference between "icing" or a "power play." If someone observed my behavior at that hockey game, they would have thought that I had a complete understanding of the game because I cheered and booed at the appropriate times. In reality, I naturally just followed the cues of the crowd to determine when I should cheer and clap or display displeasure.

Because humans instinctually follow behavioral cues, setting a tone of good behavior should be the foundation of your class. Every time that I've supervised a student teacher, I've explained that the most important thing they need to stress about is how they manage the classroom. If you can focus on this, everything else will fall into place.

On the first few days of school, many teachers have "getting to know you" activities set up for students. You could play a "getting to know you" bingo activity, which lists a variety of hobbies and activities that the students may be interested in. Each student navigates through the room trying to get signatures of students who have those hobbies. The first student to get a "cover-all" bingo wins a prize of your choosing. You could also just have the students fill out index cards with their birthday or a list of each student's hobbies. If you have a particular difficult student, you could make a connection with that student by pulling their index card and researching more on their interests and taking some time to talk to that student about their hobbies. Focus on having excitement and inflection in your voice when speaking to that student to show your enthusiasm of their hobbies.

Something that is all too common in education is that teachers will sometimes let their anger and emotions get the best of them. It's important to remember, regardless of if you're teaching kindergarten or the twelfth grade, you're the professional adult, and the students are children. You should never let their comments, disrespectful looks, or bad attitude get to you. Trust me, my first couple years of teaching, it was hard for me to keep my cool sometimes when you had that one student who would cuss and blow up for no particular reason at all. After all, it's human instinct to react to this situation. Kids go through tremendous growth changes in their short 18 years, both physically and emotionally. Considering that you're probably a teacher yourself or studying to become one, you've taken countless hours of psychology courses and you understand the complexity of a child's behavior and changes that they'll endure throughout the early stages of their life. Once you get out of a University and into your own classroom, it's so easy to forget things that we've learned to prepare us to deal with student's shifts in behavior. Kids (especially adolescents) have mood swings that come and go. I've had students who were next to fighting mad after they broke a rule and were told that they would be required to attend a lunch detention. By the next day, they were happy and giving me a high five on the way out of class. You have to remember to leave your emotions out of it and understand that students will have mood swings, will get angry, and it's nothing personal. No matter who the teacher is, there will be some students who have bad days. Disassociate yourself from being invested in arguing with a child. You also never know what situation that child is going through. Their parents could have just announced that they're divorcing the night before. They could be hungry because they cannot afford a nutritious breakfast and have too much pride to apply for assistance through the school, or they could be running on a few hours of sleep because they had to babysit their brothers and sisters while their parents are working a second or third job just to put food on the table. You have to take into consideration that each child's situation differs and might not be in the best of circumstances. Stay calm, take a deep breath, and don't let your emotions get in the way of disciplining students.

It's also important to have an arsenal of consequences. No two children are the same. I've seen effective methods from several teachers in different states throughout the years. One example that another teacher used was issuing definitions (write-offs) for inappropriate behavior. His justification was to give the definitions of the current chapter he was covering in the book for further enrichment of the content that was being taught. He would make the students write the definitions in the chapter three times each. I'm personally not a fan of this method because the student may begin to think that school work is synonymous with being a punishment. Was it effective for this teacher? Yes. Speaking with coaches, club sponsors, issuing lunch detentions (the students still eat lunch but in silence), and the most effective consequence is contacting parents.

Parental involvement is a key factor in student success. Parents are powerful. When I was young, I had a three wheeler that I rode throughout our farm. I like to use the analogy of a three wheeler to student success. If one wheel is missing, the three wheeler will not move, and if a wheel is loose, you need to fix it. Each wheel can be representative of a three part model of success. One wheel is the teacher, the second wheel is the student, and the third wheel is represented as the parents. Parental involvement should be a must in order to successfully manage your class. If you have an open house, make a point to get e-mail addresses, phone numbers, and any contact information you can from parents. You can e-mail parents and update them on general assignments, tests, projects, and other class news that parents would be interested in. Communication improves your relationship with parents and just the fact that you stay in contact with parents is enough for some students to never act up in your class. They know that you have a direct means of contact with their parents and many students will not act inappropriately when they understand that there will be a consequence at school and at home for acting out in class. It's a fact that some students may not have the fear of having backlash once they arrive home from school after acting out in class. Be clear when addressing the rules that have been broken with each student and why they're receiving the consequence. Every student has a method which will make them reflect and feel remorse for breaking the rule, so be sure to stay persistent in finding out what works for your students. You may need to use a variety of consequences for repeat offenders until you find what's effective. Just don't give up.

By being firm, yet fair and reasonable with your rules that have been established, your students will naturally have a behavior that you seek. Too many teachers want to run a dictatorship when they begin teaching. Research how many people flee or attempt to flee countries that are led by dictators. This idea of running a classroom in this manner is terrible. My first year of teaching was a roller coaster ride. I couldn't find my teaching "personality." I wanted to be the "cool" teacher one day and the next day, I wanted to be the extremely strict disciplinarian. You need to be reasonable as a teacher. If you're too relaxed, it will backfire on you as well. You need to have a happy medium where students know their boundaries and that it's ok for them to feel relaxed and comfortable while learning in your class, but at the same time, they're very much aware that you will stick to your rules and the consequences that you have established. During the first couple weeks of school, it's inevitable that a student will break a rule in class. I take this time to address the rule(s) that have been broken, and I may issue that student a lunch detention. This will curb future problems with the individual student, but I have also completely stopped class to address the student, and the situation makes an example and reminder to the other students that I'm serious about the rules and their learning. When a rule is broken, you shouldn't just threaten a consequence but should execute it quick and efficiently, so that the rest of the class may move on with the learning material.

As time goes on, you will get better and better at distinguishing discipline problems as they arise. We certainly didn't walk into our classrooms on day one of our teaching careers and instantly run a tight ship. It's like anything else in life that you try to get good at; it will take practice as well as trial and error to discover which techniques work best for you.

So many students never receive any justification of why they are learning. They're simply told to "go to school and get good grades." Rarely does anyone explain to the students any reasoning on why it's important to receive good grades, what scholarships are, why a GPA is important, etc. At the elementary level, don't just explain how to solve a math problem; explain how this will become useful for everyday life. Ask the students about situations where they think they may be able to utilize things you're learning about.

Take some time to tie in the lesson to real life situations. Justify the purpose of the lessons. The students who are on the verge of "not caring" or "not willing to try" will have an extra motivational burst of ambition when they realize that the lesson could be beneficial to them not only for the next test, but for life in general.

CHAPTER 9

MANAGING THE CLASSROOM, OUTSIDE THE CLASSROOM

MATTHEW OGLES

So you're set. You've got the whole year planned out ready to go. Classroom set up perfectly? Check. Opening strategies? Check. Group work plans? Check. Interactive classroom? Check. You've literally got it all and planned out for maximum classroom management effectiveness...but one thing most teachers forget about it how to manage the classroom outside of the classroom itself once the year has started. While creating management inside the classroom is the main priority, management techniques outside the classroom can have almost as much impact. This goes back to the lesson in Chapter One "Breaking the Barrier," get the students to realize that you are more than a teacher and establish a personal connection with them and let them know you actually care about them (making a difference in your students lives is why you went into teaching to begin with, so let it show). Once this connection is established they will not want to jeopardize a good friendship just like anyone else, and, therefore, their behavior will always be its best for you.

The first way to help establish management outside the classroom is to coach a team. The students only get to know you for the short time that you have them in class everyday and vice versa. They know you're there to help them anyway you can, but some students may still see you as just a teacher. If you coach a sport, then the students get to see you invest your own personal time into helping them. They know that you care about more than just their test scores; they know you care about seeing them succeed in other ways. This may seem small; but, once they know you care, their behavior immediately increases. But caching does more that just cementing the idea you care about them; coaching allows the students to respect you and your wisdom in multiple areas. When I coached, students never once questioned my ideas on the field; they knew we both wanted to win the game, and I was there to help. Once they got used to doing this on the field it transferred into the classroom at the same time. It was odd to see it, but the behavior of my students was actually getting better because of what I was doing outside the classroom! The ball player students set the example, and the rest of the class soon followed. Coaching really does make inside the classroom easier; yet, so many teachers don't want to invest the time into coaching because the money isn't good enough. If those teachers could just see what a difference it makes in the classroom, they would be begging to have coaching positions.

Now, some of you reading this book are probably saying, "Well shoot, I don't know how to coach a sport." Well, fear not! All the advantages described in the previous paragraph can still be taken advantage of by leading a club! I have coached both soccer and football and reaped all the advantages management wise described, but I saw just as many rewards when I started being a club leader. I have been associated with multiple clubs during my years teaching, and every time I'm involved I can tell once again what I am doing outside the classroom is affecting what I do inside it. When students see me stay after school to help them lead a club of what they are interested in, they immediately gain more respect for me. They see that I once again care about them, and they want to show their appreciation by behaving during my class. Deep down every kid knows what it means to behave; therefore, since they like and respect you they will make sure they behave during your classroom.

The best club that I have ever helped lead is hands down History Team. Every year I get the kids to take a test around Christmas time as a qualifying test. The top ten scores all become members of the history team. I wait until Christmas for a reason. I tell the kids at the beginning of the year about the team and promise them, a free day out-of-school trip, free t-shirt, after school fun, and many other things. The kids all get excited but know they have to work hard until Christmas to get in it. This helps all students behavior until Christmas because they want to hear my lessons in order to be more prepared for the qualifying test, and even after Christmas because they want to see how the rest of the United States history story line turns out. But those who make the team are like the athletes I have coached. They know I care about them and want them to succeed in multiple areas and, therefore, they behave extra well in class to respect that.

Now it may come across here to either coach a team or lead a club just to reap behavior benefits, but that's honestly not what it's all about. While this does help behaviors, it also allows you to fulfill your original reason for becoming a teacher…to help students and make a difference in their lives. The bonds I've made with students on teams and in clubs are one of the best parts of the job.

The first two ways to establish good classroom management outside the classroom both take a good bit of effort. I'm not going to lie, I have spent hours and hours on the field coaching and not everyone has time for that. If that is an option for the boat you're in, just simply strive to go to some of the sport games. This works best if you are a small school because the students will see that you've attended. The students' work extraordinarily hard to be on those teams and compete and when they see you at the games, it shows that you care about them. If they see that you care about them and the things that they put effort into, then they will in return care about your lessons and show you respect. Plus you get to see a free sports game! But going to sports games also gives you another advantage to classroom management...you get to meet the parents.

Being in contact with your students' parents is hands down one of the best management techniques that I've come across. I realize this doesn't seem that unconventional on the surface because we all know, being teachers, that it is standard to call parents when the students misbehave. However, think how many times you've called a parent and they began to attack you because of what their child did and how you were wrong to punish them. Imagine calling the parents and having them take your side...it's easy to get to this point and it also makes the classroom management easier because the students will want to behave for you and their parents. In order to get the parents to take your side when you call, make sure you know the parents from earlier in the year. There are so many ways to do this. As briefly mentioned in the last paragraph, meet them at the games and get to know them. If the parents know you're a good person who means well, then they will take your side when you call to report bad behavior on their child. Also, make calling the parents a common thing. Every week make it a habit to call every parent in one of your classes, and then just rotate classes each week. When making these phone calls tell them what's going on in your class and make them feel involved. Also discuss their individual child and how he's doing in your class and be sure and tell something positive. If the parent knows how your class operates and once again sees that you care for their child, then they will support you. If they support you, then they will tell their child to behave for you while they are at school. If the child doesn't behave and you have to make the phone call, the parent is almost certain to support you. Parental support is one of the most powerful management tools that a teacher can use, and the only way to make sure you have it is to maintain constant contact with the parents.

Management outside the classroom really just boils down to one thing, caring. Get out there in the community and let the students and parents know that you truly care for them and their child. If they see that you truly care, then the students will want to behave for you to maintain your support and friendship. Likewise when the parents see you caring for their child, they will also encourage their student to behave for you and do well in your class. Being a teacher is a full time job and being most successful at it may just take a bit of your free time to make it work.

UNCONVENTIONAL CHALLENGE

Take the plunge this week. Sit down with your roll and call every parent on the list. It is going to be a lot of work, but I promise it will be worth it in the long run. Tell the parent what is going on in your class academically as well as about their child's performance. They will be happy to hear from you and will be so much more open when you have to call about problems.

Check out the school's calendar. You know it is on the website or in the office, or better yet, ask a student. Just find out when the next sporting event is at your school and attend it. It is a small step, but it will show the students you care as well as helping to establish parental contact.

Evaluate if you have extra time after school. Is there a sport or club you could help lead? Take a stroll down to the principal's office and let him know you want to help out. It will help your management enormously in the long run so go ahead...take the plunge.

CHAPTER 10

DON'T LET THE LIGHTS GO OUT

BRENT BOGAN

We've all had those days in the middle of the winter season when the sun goes down in the early evening, and we lose all energy and motivation for everything. The only motivation that we do have is walking to the bedroom to meet a soft pillow that's calling our name. By design, humans have a circadian rhythm that triggers us to rise with the sun and fall asleep with the sunset. Sometimes leaving for school when it's dark outside and arriving home when it's dark makes us tired in our teaching.

Too often, teachers get into a routine and lose their energy. This is when they "fall asleep" on their students. By instinct, humans adapt to routines, and once they become adjusted to a particular routine, it becomes a habit. It's important to keep the energy level high in your classroom. A highly energetic, motivated teacher is reflective of someone with great classroom management. Think about a public speaker or teacher that you've had with high energy and enthusiasm. Now compare that person to someone who was monotone and bland. More than likely, you whispered to others around you when the presenter with the bland personality spoke or maybe you were day dreaming about all of the fun and exciting things you were going to do once you could escape from the speaker who's personality was dry. Now think about the teacher or speaker that was charismatic and spoke with great excitement and inflection in his/her voice. You probably listened to every word he/she spoke because of his/her enthusiasm and you more than likely didn't have an opportunity to doodle the latest Picasso version of stick figures in your notebook because you were so consumed with paying attention to the energetic speaker.

Teaching should never get to a point of redundancy. Teachers have the power to create the way their lessons are taught, and few careers allow workers to determine the flow and pace of their day. As Matthew mentioned earlier in the book, if you're not having fun, the students are not having fun. Keeping the energy level high is part of keeping it fun.

Students of every grade level have lots of energy, and they need a teacher that can equally dish out a great deal of charisma to keep up with them. There are several great leaders who have risen to power throughout history. Many of those leaders had one common characteristic. The characteristic that they usually possessed was the ability to be exciting when they spoke publicly.

In chapter 7, I made reference to how Garth Brooks sells out shows consecutively year after year. Garth once explained that before each and every show, he would climb to the farthest seat from the stage in the arena, would sit in that seat, turn around to the stage, and reflect on how that person would be entertained so far away from where the music was being played. His goal was to not only captivate those who paid extra for the floor seats, but to entertain each and every concert-goer equally, regardless of the cost.

In many ways, teachers should treat their class-room like a concert. Put yourself in the seat of the student. Would the lesson that you're teaching capti-vate you? A major component of classroom management is keeping your students motivated and excited about your class, so many teachers get "com-fortable" and into a routine of mediocrity teaching. Although your students have not purchased a ticket to a concert, the tax payers or parents (depending on if you teach at a public or private school) have paid for you to educate the students.

Everyone finds self-motivation and drive in a variety of ways. For each teacher, it may take some-thing different than the next to motivate them and maintain excitement in the class. Let's say that you're motivated by knowing that the students are learning and appreciate your efforts. You could keep an old shoe box full of letters, Christmas cards, colored pictures, and anything else that students hand you through the years. You can refer to this box if you ever question if you're in the right profession. If you just started teaching, you could give the students a report card to fill out on you. This will give you an opportunity to figure out what's effective for the students, what's enjoyable for the students, and what you could maybe omit from your teaching. At the same time, you're going to have some words of encouragement from students that will motivate you on those days where you walk into school, and five cups of coffee wouldn't wake you up enough to be motivated about the day.

Here are some daily affirmations you can use to self-motivate:

1. The average teacher will teach 180 days in a year and have 185 days off. Know that a break is always around to corner for mental and physical rest: fall break, holidays, Christmas break, spring break, and summer break.

2. Understand that your career is more than the typical punching of a time clock, producing or shipping a product, and then clocking out after the work is done. There are some people in the public who view teachers as glorified babysitters. With all of the new education legislation and new expectations that are required from teachers, you know there is nothing further from the truth, (In the last decade, there have tremendous changes in our American public education system. Students are being pushed to new levels. Kindergarteners now have to focus on learning a second language and pre-algebra instead of playing and having naptime. High schools are now using tracking systems to appropriate place students based on their learning abilities. Gone are the days of teachers taking an afternoon nap at their desk and showing videos all day). Regardless of public perception, you are making a huge impact in the lives of our future, and your students will learn things from you that they will take with them the rest of their lives.

3. You must see darkness before you see the light at the end of the tunnel. Throughout the year, you may be swamped with meetings, scheduling conferences with parents and fielding hundreds of e-mails each week, and there could be a thousand things you're reflecting on that occurred throughout the day. Remember that your busy times will come and go in waves.

4. You can and will succeed at the goals that you seek for yourself and your students.

5. You are an effective teacher and disciplinarian.

Another method of motivation may be money. Assuming you're in the field of education, money was probably not a major factor that influenced you to enter into the world of teaching; otherwise, you would've applied your college efforts towards a more lucrative career. If you've taken the time to read this book, it's evident that you more than likely became a teacher to make a difference in the lives of children and teach them skills, content, and moral lessons that they will maintain throughout their lives.

However, let's say that you make a teaching salary of $50,000 (this figure is actually below the national average for teaching salaries at the time of this writing). Now, let's assume that you teach for 180 days a year. Many schools average a seven hour day.

(Annual Salary)/(Days Teaching)=Daily Salary
$50,000 ÷ 180 = $277.77

(Daily Salary)/(Hours Spent Teaching)=Hourly Salary
$277.77 ÷ 7 = $39.68 an hour

So for each hour that you teach your students, just remind yourself that you've been chosen and hired to inspire, motivate, and educate students at the rate of nearly $40 an hour. Not many careers at the time of this writing pay a salary this high, nor do they pay to do something as noble as teaching.

Now I know that this does not include everything that's withdrawn from your checks, nor does it include planning lessons outside of school, stopping by the teacher supply store on your days off, or arriving at school two hours early to grade that large stack of papers that seems to rival the height and magnitude of Mount Everest. The point I'm trying to make is that on the days when you feel like you just don't have it in you, keep this fact in mind -- you don't just owe it to the tax-paying community; you owe it to the kids.

It's important to find a teacher who can be a mentor and a confidant. You can vent your concerns and frustrations, as well as collaborate on what is working well in each of your classes. It will help you grow as a teacher and not build up as much stress when you have someone else whom you can rely on. Another piece of advice is to greet your students at your classroom door before class begins. Think about a retail business or restaurant where you feel welcome or comfortable. It's likely that the retail or restaurant establishment that you thought of may have a greeter who welcomes you when you enter through the front door. Successful business models show that people want to be greeted in a friendly manner, and your classroom should be no different. Students want to feel welcome when entering your room, and it's the very first impression that the students will have of your class each day.

We sincerely hope that this book has been of help to you and that you will walk away from reading this with a few new techniques that you will utilize within your classroom. Remember to stay involved and in contact with parents. Not only will it improve school and community involvement; it will help student's grades and will help minimize classroom disruptions by students.

Set high expectations for your students. If you teach a college preparatory course or and advanced placement class, this idea is always intact but many forget to have ambitious goals for the students who might not be in these classes. If you keep your students engaged, continuously check for understanding, and keep discipline problems to a minimum, your students are bound to excel.

The last piece of advice I would like to give you is to not give up. Classroom management does not come naturally for anyone. It takes work, clever thought, and persistence. One of my former mentors explained to me that your first year of teaching feels like you're drowning, the second year is comparable to treading water, and your third year you will begin to swim. Far too many teachers have great teaching methods and the knowledge and education to be a great teacher, but they give up when they don't make classroom management a foundation for their class. By including some of the methods in this book, we hope that management will be the least of your worries when your students feel respected, are comfortable, and are having fun while learning. When you teach, it's important to not let the lights go out on your energy and teaching philosophies. It's so easy to get into a comfortable routine and ease up on the rules. You have to treat each day and every hour with as much importance as the next. If you go to the computer lab, recess, an assembly, etc., you need to communicate your behavioral expectations and consequences each and every time. Many teachers repeat the same lesson year after year, class after class. The beauty of being a teacher is that you not only have the ability to tap into your students' creativity, you can also use your creativity to keep lessons interesting, unique, and exciting. If you keep your excitement high, the amount of discipline problems will be low.

UNCONVENTIONAL CHALLENGE

Whether it's the policy of your school or if it's because you're setting up your classroom, most teachers arrive at school well before the first student takes a step off of the school bus in the morning. Take this opportunity to not only prepare your classroom materials, but to also prepare yourself. I'd like to challenge you to take a seat in the back of your classroom and visualize how you will "entertain" or teach to that student who will sit in that seat for the day. What will you do differently to make sure that every student in each seat will benefit from your lesson? Half of the battle of classroom management is using reverse psychology and thinking in the mind of the student to win over their appropriate behavior.

CHAPTER 11

SOME EXTRA TOOLS

OF THE TRADE

BRENT BOGAN

Classroom management is a topic that cannot ever be covered within the confines of a book. The causes for disruption and misconduct are unlimited, and the situations are often times unique. Just when a teacher thinks that they've seen it all, something new and sometimes unbelievable will happen. Just as with academics, no two children learn in the same way; with discipline, no two students may respond identically with the consequences administered for the misconduct.

In this bonus chapter, we'll cover a few additional methods that may help teachers with their pursuit of managing behaviors at school. As previously mentioned in this book, developing a teacher-student relationship and finding commonalities and connections with students is a very useful way to not only build a positive classroom climate and culture, but to also reduce the amount of discipline issues.

If there is one particular student or even if there's a group of students who continuously has issues with being defiant, talking out of turn, or just being off task and inattentive, there are methods of building a bond with students. Those methods are often referred to as the 5X5 or the 2X10 methods. In my experience as a teacher and as a school administrator, I personally think that the 2X10 (two by ten) method is the most effective of the two. The way that the 2X10 method works is that for a cumulative amount of two minutes each day, for ten consecutive days, a teacher, counselor, or administrator will speak with a student about non-academically related topics.

The 2X10 method conversations should consist of topics that do not include a correction or a direction. An example could include greeting students at your door and breaking the ice with a student who has exhibited signs of negative behavior by initiating a conversation by complimenting his Michael Jordan shoes and then discussing what other sports that they may like. If that conversation lasts for one minute, speak to the student again later in the day to fill up the two minutes. This should be repeated for the next nine consecutive days. If you have multiple students who are behavioral concerns, once this method has been used with the student who is the ring leader of misconduct within your classroom, the method can be used again for the next student.

Often times when a student is starting to show up on the radar, as an administrator, I will sometimes call him/her out into the hallway and take a walk down the hall and initiate a conversation with a student that doesn't involve a correction or a direction. Having a conversation while walking down the hall doesn't involve squaring your shoulders with a student and is not intimidating. At my school, there are no physical education classes held between 8:00 and 8:45, so this is an opportunity for me and some troubled students to shoot some basketball in the morning in a non-confrontational way. Often times, students act out to seek attention, as they are not receiving any attention at home. If basketball isn't an option and walking down the hall and having the student assist you with an errand isn't feasible, making a point to speak with the student one-on-one while your class is engaged in an activity that allows you to walk around the room and check for understanding is certainly a prime time to try the 2X10 method.

For elementary grades, if students are having issues of keeping their hands to themselves, being defiant, or is having trouble with outbursts, then creating a "cool down" area in the room will allow students to de-escalate their behaviors. A cool down area is in a designated area of the room that is isolated from other students. The cool down area can include cards that give students directives on calming themselves down. These cards can include peaceful pictures of the ocean, snow-capped mountains, or other serene scenes of nature. There can also be instructions such as pretending to "slowly smell a flower and then blow out a candle." These breathing techniques permit the extra oxygen to produce a calming agent.

Another activity that can take place in the cool down area is to allow students to write in a journal about how they were feeling before and leading up to the incident that caused them to be moved. This journal can help the student reflect in what is causing them to become emotionally disturbed or act out during class. Furthermore, the students can write about what action steps they would like to take to improve their behavior moving forward. If a student can self-assess and articulate what's causing the behavior, that's half of the battle to finding solutions to curbing the behaviors.

Behavior tracking sheets is also great for students in K-8. If a student is consistently having issues with a particular behavior, the behavior tracking sheets provide data as well as attainable goals that students create each day to help progress towards making improvements in the way that they behave during the school day. Behavior tracking logs work best when there are at most two to three behaviors that need to be focused on at one time. For example, if a student has ongoing issues with not raising his/her hand to gain permission to speak and has issues with remaining seated during class, the behavior sheet will list those two behaviors. The student will check in each morning with the teacher to determine what his/her overall goal is for the day. For example, if the student believes that he/she will be able to stay seated for 12 out of 14 thirty-minute periods throughout the day, the goal will be written by the teacher and the student will place their signature on the behavior chart sheet. The student will keep the chart in his/her possession throughout the day. Every 30 minutes, the teacher will mark the student's page if he/she did or didn't meet the behavior goal for the 30-minute duration. At the end of the day, if the student met his/her goal, the student can be rewarded with an extrinsic reward, such as a sticker, candy, or a positive phone call from the teacher to the child's parents.

Once a student has met his/her goal for several weeks, the behavior chart can be broken down to having the student reach the goal every hour or four times per day, until eventually the good behaviors have become habitual and the behavior chart is no longer needed. Just as there is an extraordinary amount of research stating the benefits of students tracking their academic progress data, the same ownership and pride takes place when students see their progress and improvements.

For students who become upset and may begin throwing desks, chairs, and school supplies, proprioceptive input exercises may work for children. When a student is becoming angry and it's escalating to the point of where the student is getting physically upset, a student could be called into the hallway. With no other students around, they can press their hands against the wall and push as if they were doing a push up on the wall. This muscle resistance is called proprioceptive input, puts pressure on the midline, and in turn creates a calming effect for students.

Two to three folders is another method of calming students. If a student is becoming upset, the teacher can ask the student to go down the hall to another teacher's classroom to grab three folders. The other teacher knows that this is code for the student needing three minutes of time to cool down. The other teacher will kindly ask the student to patiently wait in the back of the room until they can find the three folders. This allows students time to calm themselves before returning back to class and prevents further disruption.

Finally, it's important that students correlate the punishment to the negative action. If a student misbehaves in the cafeteria, an assigned seat for a couple of days will provide the student opportunity to think and reflect about making good future decisions. If students do not complete their homework, an academic recess in lieu of their regularly scheduled recess could be an alternative, assuming it's not a regular occurrence. Schools may be the last opportunity that students have to learn about following rules and conforming to how one should act in society. It's a great responsibility that we have as educators to make sure that we underscore the rules and values of a school, to reflect the expectations of the real world, and to ensure

that we have a well-managed classroom that's conducive to high levels of learning.

99997734R00083

Made in the USA
Columbia, SC
14 July 2018